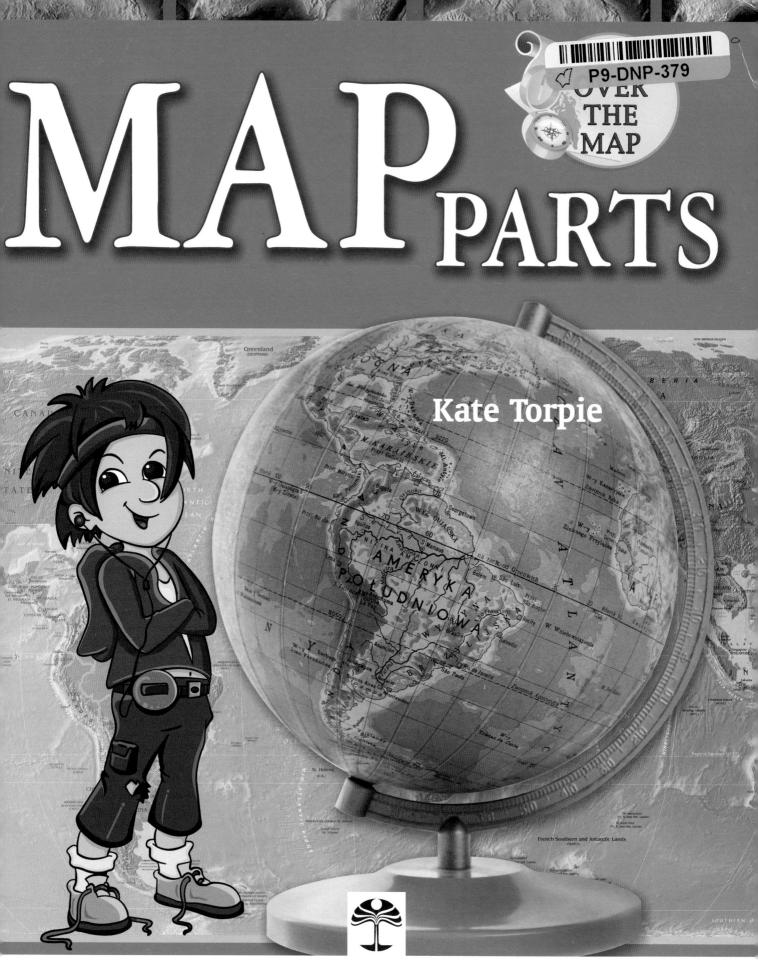

MAP PARTS

ALL OVER THE MAP

Kate Torpie

Crabtree Publishing Company

www.crabtreebooks.com

Crabtree Publishing Company

www.crabtreebooks.com

Author: Kate Torpie
Coordinating editor: Chester Fisher
Series editor: Scholastic Ventures
Project editor: Robert Walker
Editor: Reagan Miller
Proofreaders: Molly Aloian, Crystal Sikkens
Production coordinator: Katherine Kantor
Prepress technicians: Katherine Kantor, Ken Wright
Project manager: Santosh Vasudevan (Q2AMEDIA)
Art direction: Rahul Dhiman (Q2AMEDIA
Cover design: Ranjan Singh (Q2AMEDIA)
Design: Dibakar Acharjee (Q2AMEDIA)
Photo research: Sejal Sehgal Wani (Q2AMEDIA)

Photographs:
Cia.gov: p. 18
Dreamstime: Indiansummer: p. 19; Megumi: p. 21 (top)
Fotolia: Profotokris: p. 6 (top right), 30 (top right); Titimel35:
      p. 21 (bottom); Thor Jorgen Udvang: p. 30 (bottom right)
Istockphoto: Jakub Semeniuk: p. 1, 20
Jupiter Images: Imageshop: p. 11 (globe)
Map Resources: p. 28–29
NASA: p. 4, 25 (top)
Nationalatlas.gov: p. 12, 14, 15, 16–17, 31 (top right)
Shutterstock: Stasys Eidiejus: p. 22–23, 31 (top left); Cindy Hughes:
      cover (bottom right); Gabriel Moisa: cover (background)
      Pavel Losevsky: p. 5, 30 (top left); Noah Strycker: p. 26
United States Federal Government: p. 1 (background), 24–25, 31 (bottom)
Usgs.gov: cover (background)

Illustrations:
Q2AMedia

Library and Archives Canada Cataloguing in Publication

Torpie, Kate, 1974-
      Map parts / Kate Torpie.

(All over the map)
Includes index.
ISBN 978-0-7787-4268-5 (bound).--ISBN 978-0-7787-4273-9 (pbk.)

      1. Map reading--Juvenile literature. 2. Maps--Juvenile literature.
I. Title. II. Series: All over the map (St. Catharines, Ont.)

GA105.6.T67 2008   j912.01'4   C2008-903495-3

Library of Congress Cataloging-in-Publication Data

Torpie, Kate, 1974-
      Map parts / Kate Torpie.
            p. cm. -- (All over the map)
      Includes index.
      ISBN-13: 978-0-7787-4273-9 (pbk. : alk. paper)
      ISBN-10: 0-7787-4273-3 (pbk. : alk. paper)
      ISBN-13: 978-0-7787-4268-5 (reinforced library binding : alk. paper)
      ISBN-10: 0-7787-4268-7 (reinforced library binding : alk. paper)
      1. Maps--Juvenile literature. I. Title. II. Series.

      GA105.6.T669 2009
      912--dc22
                                                            2008023526

Crabtree Publishing Company

www.crabtreebooks.com   1-800-387-7650

Published in Canada
Crabtree Publishing
616 Welland Ave.
St. Catharines, Ontario
L2M 5V6

Published in the United States
Crabtree Publishing
PMB16A
350 Fifth Ave., Suite 3308
New York, NY 10118

Published in the United Kingdom
Crabtree Publishing
White Cross Mills
High Town, Lancaster
LA1 4XS

Published in Australia
Crabtree Publishing
386 Mt. Alexander Rd.
Ascot Vale (Melbourne)
VIC 3032

CONTENTS

Where in the World Am I?

Where in the World Am I?
At My House!

Hello, my name is Max. Today in school, I learned about **maps**. A map is a representation of a place. People draw maps or print them on paper. Maps are tools to help us find where we are and where we are going. Now that I learned about maps, I can tell you exactly where I am!

▲ *I live on planet Earth. So do you! That doesn't mean we are in the same place. Where exactly on Earth am I?*

▲ I am in my bedroom. This is a picture of my bedroom.
I decorated it myself. But where exactly is my bedroom?

The parts of a map help us understand how to read the information.

All maps have **titles**. Titles tell you what the map will show you. This map is called "My House." That's because the map will show you where all the rooms in my house are!

▲ *This is the house where I live.*

MY HOUSE

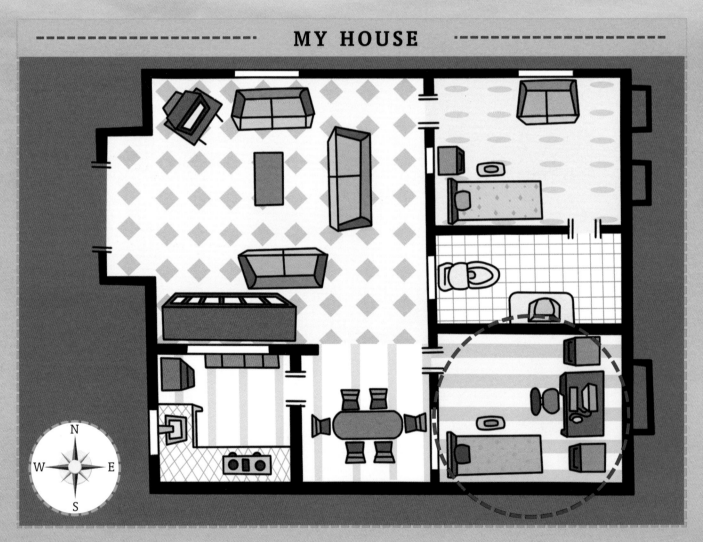

▲ *Here is my room.*

A **compass rose** is a part on a map. The compass rose is used to show the positions of north, south, east, and west. It is usually placed in the lower left-hand corner of a map. The compass rose is used to locate places on a map using direction.

My house is in a neighborhood near the park and the beach. Look at the map below. The park is east of my neighborhood.

Can you find my neighborhood? Use the compass rose to help you find the direction east. Can you see the park east of my neighborhood?

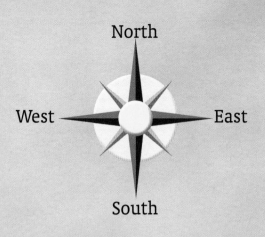

This is a large compass rose. Can you find two smaller ones on these two pages?

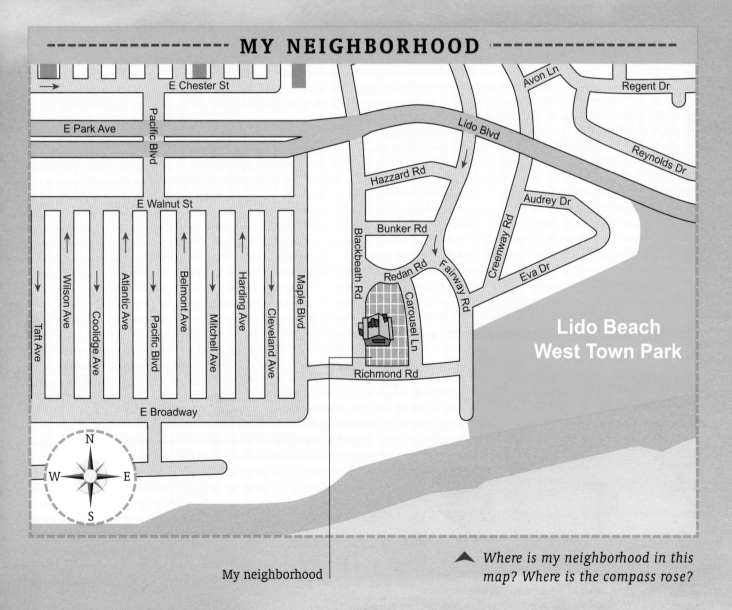

▲ *Where is my neighborhood in this map? Where is the compass rose?*

Where in the World Am I? In My City!

My neighborhood is exactly in the city of Long Beach, New York. I'll try to draw a map of the busy part of my city to show you. First, I'll title it: The Busy Section of Long Beach, NY.

You can see all the places that matter most to me on this map. I labeled my house, my school, my favorite stores, and our two main streets. They sure took a long time to draw!

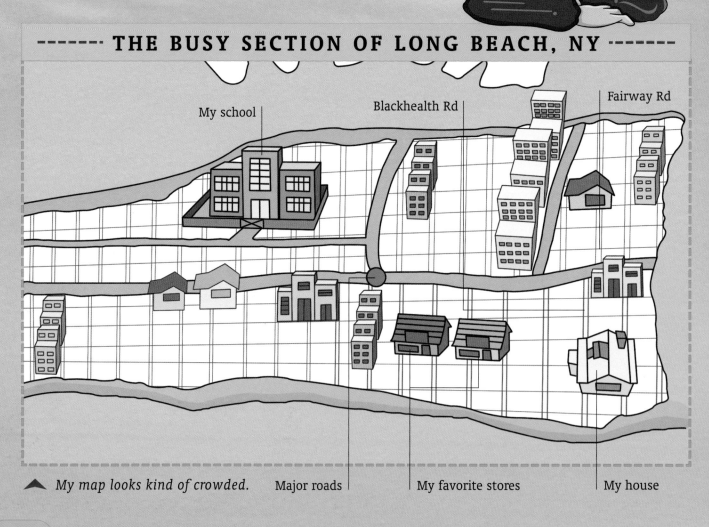

------- THE BUSY SECTION OF LONG BEACH, NY -------

Fairway Rd

Blackhealth Rd

My school

▲ *My map looks kind of crowded.*   Major roads   My favorite stores   My house

This map shows the same information that my drawing did. It's a lot easier to read! That's because they used **symbols** and a **legend** instead of labeling all the places. A map has a legend to explain the meaning of each symbol used on the map. If a map has a symbol on it, it needs to have a legend. These two map parts go together.

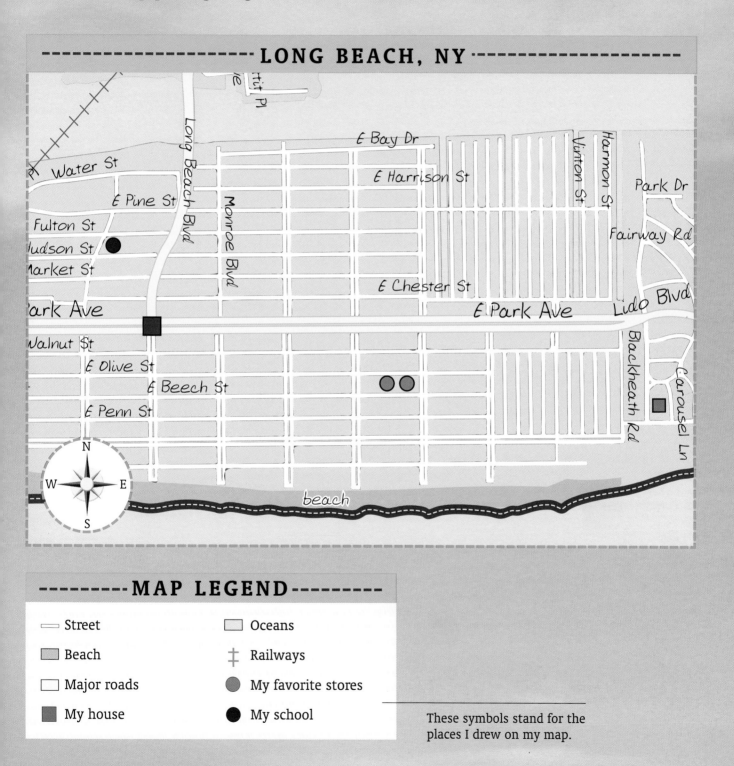

These symbols stand for the places I drew on my map.

The title of this map is "Long Beach, NY." What other map parts do you see? This map has a compass rose, legend, and symbols. There's a new map part down there—it's called a **scale**.

A map represents a large area of land. A map must be small enough to fit on a piece of paper, but it must also show the distance between places.

A scale shows you how far places are from each other.

Even color can be used as a symbol on a map. What are the blue parts on this map? Use the key to find out!

If a city is twice as large as a nearby town, the city should be twice as big as the town on the map. Scale helps you understand what the small measurements really mean.

In the Long Beach map, one inch (2.5 cm) on the map is the same as 1312 feet (400 m) on real land. In the New York City map, one inch (2.5 cm) on the map is the same as 328 feet (100 m) on real land.

The scale is usually given in metric and standard measures. No matter how you measure, you should understand the scale.

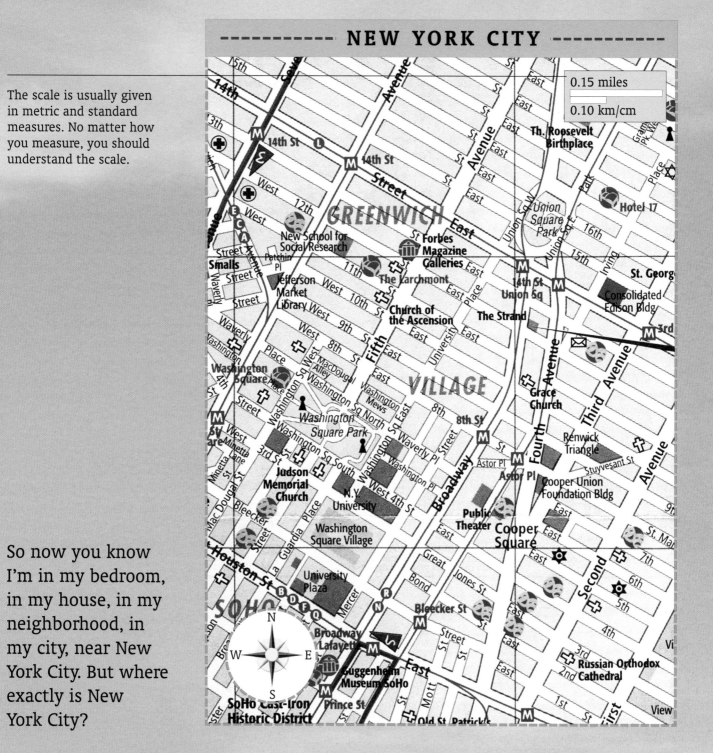

So now you know I'm in my bedroom, in my house, in my neighborhood, in my city, near New York City. But where exactly is New York City?

Where in the World Am I?
In My State!

Look at this map, titled "New York Counties" to see exactly where New York City is.

Places are outlined to show their **boundaries**. A boundary is a border that separates one place from another. This map shows the boundaries for each county. New York City is in Kings County. Long Beach is in Nassau County.

-- MAP LEGEND --

—— State Border

--- Country Border

☐ Lakes and Rivers

☐ Oceans

☐ Other States

---------------------- **NEW YORK COUNTIES** ----------------------

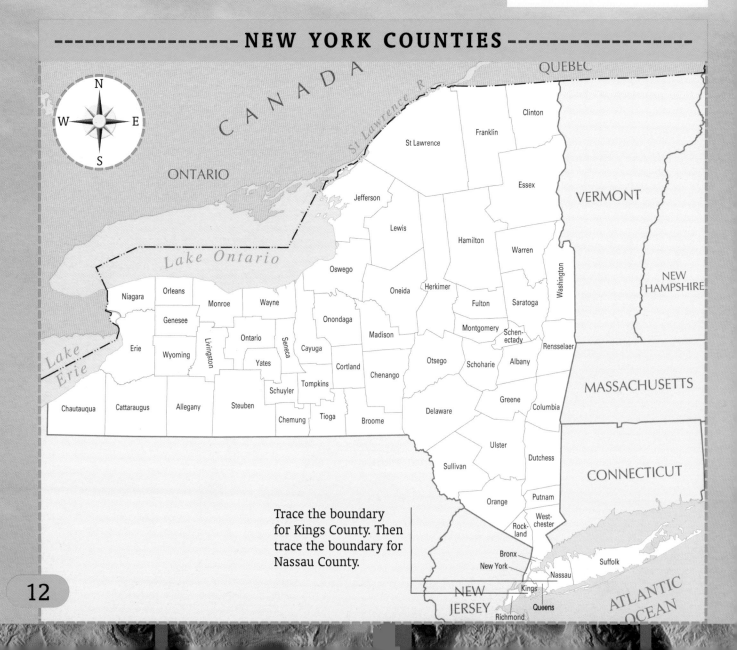

Trace the boundary for Kings County. Then trace the boundary for Nassau County.

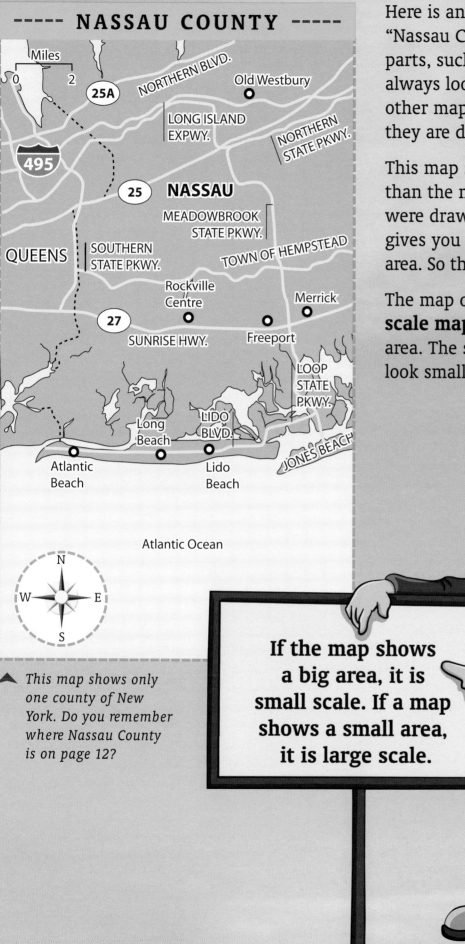

----- NASSAU COUNTY -----

Miles
0   2

25A   NORTHERN BLVD.   Old Westbury

LONG ISLAND
EXPWY.

NORTHERN
STATE PKWY.

495

25   NASSAU

MEADOWBROOK
STATE PKWY.

QUEENS   SOUTHERN
STATE PKWY.   TOWN OF HEMPSTEAD

Rockville
Centre   Merrick

27

SUNRISE HWY.   Freeport

LOOP
STATE
PKWY.

Long
Beach   LIDO
BLVD.   JONES BEACH

Atlantic
Beach   Lido
Beach

Atlantic Ocean

N
W   E
S

▲ *This map shows only one county of New York. Do you remember where Nassau County is on page 12?*

Here is another map, titled "Nassau County." Some map parts, such as compass roses, always look the same. Look at other map parts and see how they are different.

This map shows a smaller area than the map on page 12. Places were drawn larger. The scale gives you a larger view of the area. So this is a **large scale map**.

The map on page 12 is a **small scale map**. It shows a larger area. The scale makes the area look smaller.

If the map shows a big area, it is small scale. If a map shows a small area, it is large scale.

Here's another map of New York State. The title is "Highways in New York State." This map shows different information than the county map of New York State. Both of the maps may show the same state, but the information about the state is different from map to map.

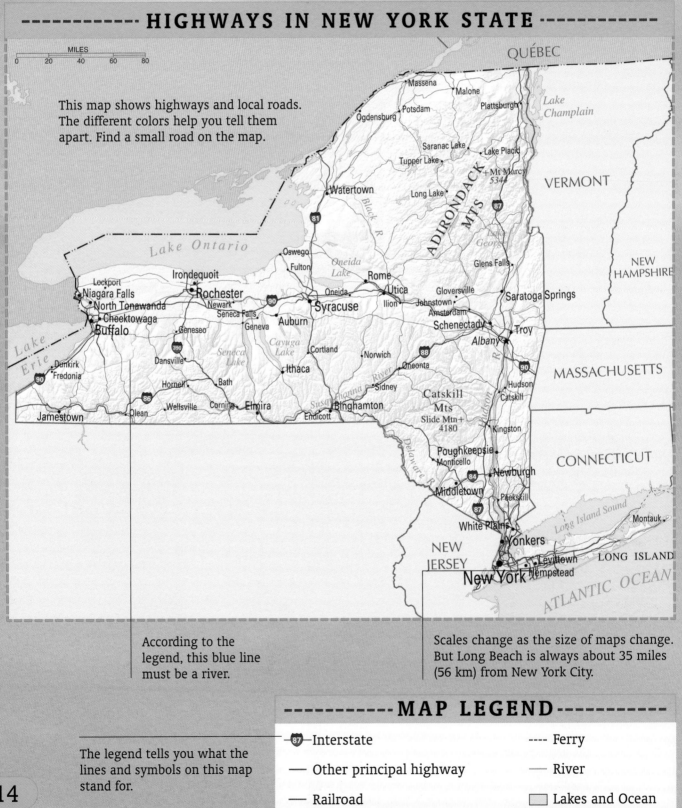

HIGHWAYS IN NEW YORK STATE

This map shows highways and local roads. The different colors help you tell them apart. Find a small road on the map.

According to the legend, this blue line must be a river.

Scales change as the size of maps change. But Long Beach is always about 35 miles (56 km) from New York City.

The legend tells you what the lines and symbols on this map stand for.

MAP LEGEND

87 Interstate   ---- Ferry

— Other principal highway   — River

— Railroad   ▭ Lakes and Ocean

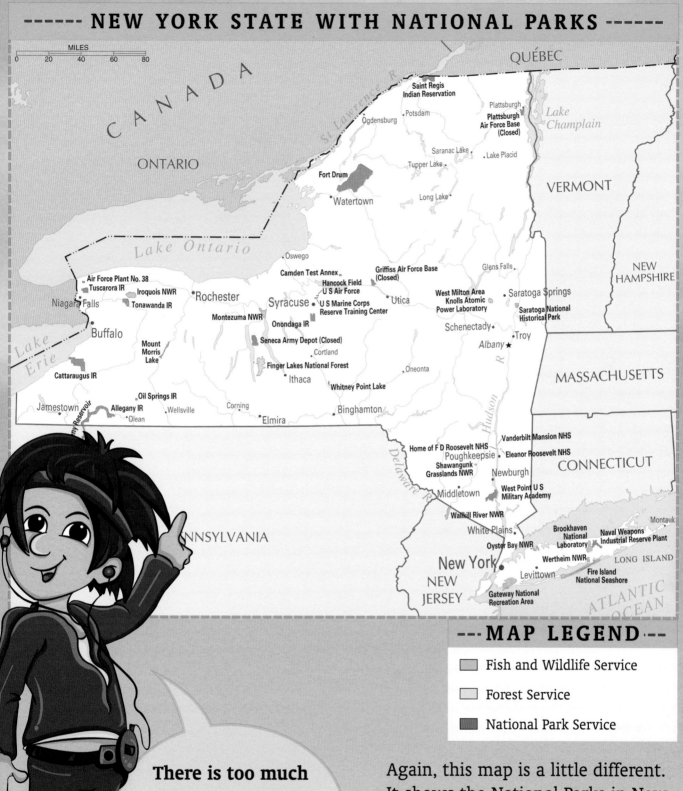

MAP LEGEND ---

Fish and Wildlife Service

Forest Service

National Park Service

There is too much information about New York State to put it all on one map!

Again, this map is a little different. It shows the National Parks in New York. Now you know that I'm in my bedroom, in my house. I am in Long Beach, which is in New York State. But where exactly is New York State?

Where in the World Am I?
In My Country!

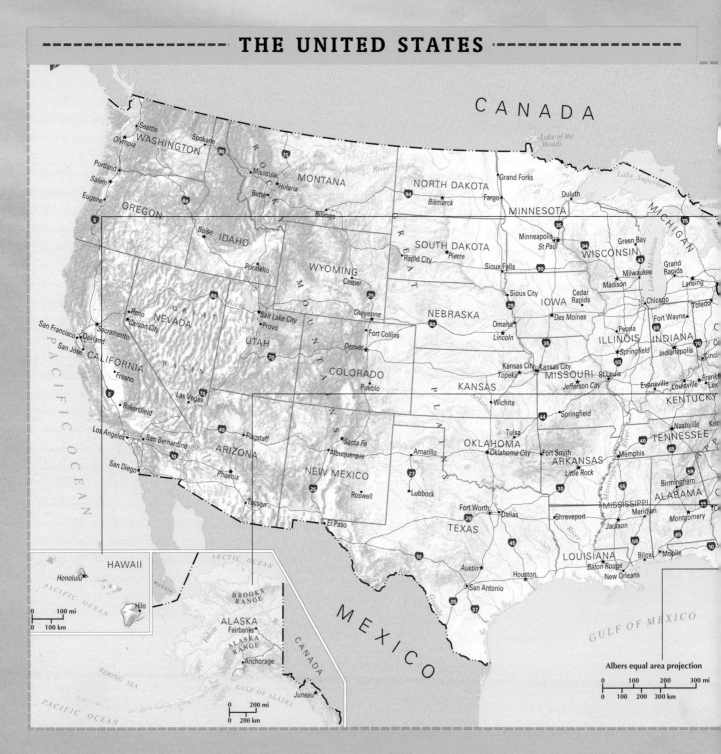

THE UNITED STATES

CANADA

WASHINGTON — Seattle, Spokane, Olympia, Portland, Salem, Eugene

OREGON

MONTANA — Missoula, Helena, Butte, Billings

NORTH DAKOTA — Grand Forks, Bismarck, Fargo

MINNESOTA — Duluth, Minneapolis, St Paul

IDAHO — Boise, Pocatello

WYOMING — Casper, Cheyenne

SOUTH DAKOTA — Rapid City, Pierre, Sioux Falls

WISCONSIN — Green Bay, Milwaukee, Madison

MICHIGAN — Grand Rapids, Lansing

NEVADA — Reno, Carson City

GREAT SALT LAKE

UTAH — Salt Lake City, Provo

COLORADO — Fort Collins, Denver, Pueblo

NEBRASKA — Omaha, Lincoln

IOWA — Sioux City, Cedar Rapids, Des Moines

ILLINOIS — Peoria, Springfield

INDIANA — Fort Wayne, Indianapolis

Chicago, Toledo

San Francisco, Oakland, San Jose, Sacramento

CALIFORNIA — Fresno, Bakersfield, Los Angeles, San Bernardino, San Diego

GREAT BASIN

Las Vegas

ARIZONA — Flagstaff, Phoenix, Tucson

NEW MEXICO — Santa Fe, Albuquerque, Roswell

KANSAS — Kansas City, Topeka, Wichita

MISSOURI — Kansas City, Jefferson City, St Louis, Springfield

Evansville, Louisville

KENTUCKY

TENNESSEE — Nashville, Memphis

Amarillo, Lubbock

OKLAHOMA — Oklahoma City, Tulsa, Fort Smith

ARKANSAS — Little Rock

Birmingham

ALABAMA — Montgomery

MISSISSIPPI — Meridian, Jackson

El Paso, Fort Worth, Dallas, Shreveport

TEXAS — Austin, San Antonio, Houston

LOUISIANA — Baton Rouge, New Orleans, Biloxi, Mobile

PACIFIC OCEAN

GULF OF MEXICO

MEXICO

Albers equal area projection

0   100   200   300 mi
0   100   200   300 km

HAWAII — Honolulu, Hilo

0   100 mi
0   100 km

PACIFIC OCEAN

ARCTIC OCEAN

RUSSIA

BROOKS RANGE

ALASKA — Fairbanks, Anchorage

ALASKA RANGE

Yukon R.

CANADA

Juneau

BERING SEA

GULF OF ALASKA

PACIFIC OCEAN

0   200 mi
0   200 km

Rio Grande

New York State is one of the United States. This map is called "The United States." It is a small scale map. It shows each of the states in our country, and gives you an idea about the shape of the land. Can you find where in the United States New York is exactly? Can you find your state?

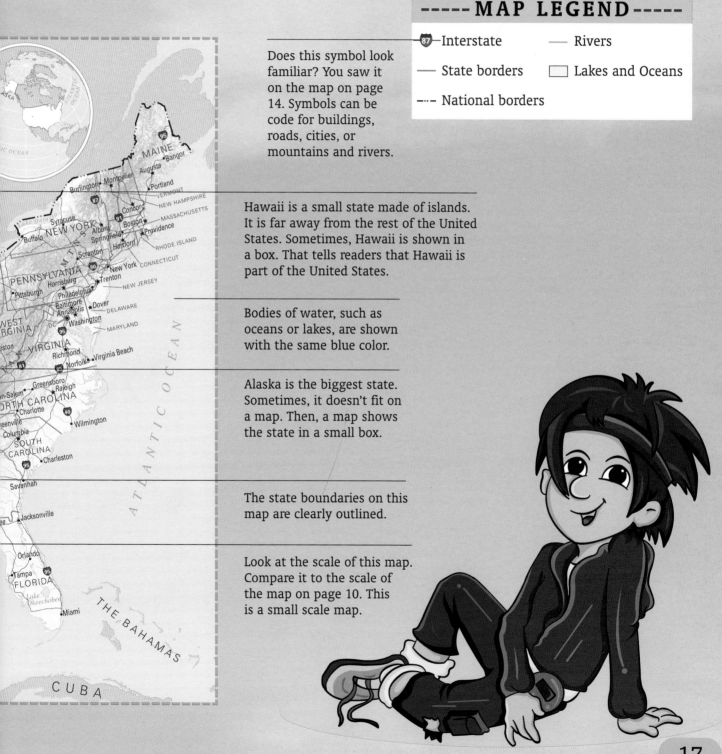

----- **MAP LEGEND** -----

🛡97 —Interstate   — Rivers

— State borders   ☐ Lakes and Oceans

–··– National borders

Does this symbol look familiar? You saw it on the map on page 14. Symbols can be code for buildings, roads, cities, or mountains and rivers.

Hawaii is a small state made of islands. It is far away from the rest of the United States. Sometimes, Hawaii is shown in a box. That tells readers that Hawaii is part of the United States.

Bodies of water, such as oceans or lakes, are shown with the same blue color.

Alaska is the biggest state. Sometimes, it doesn't fit on a map. Then, a map shows the state in a small box.

The state boundaries on this map are clearly outlined.

Look at the scale of this map. Compare it to the scale of the map on page 10. This is a small scale map.

Like the last map, this map shows the United States. But this one gives you different information. It shows the countries that border the United States.

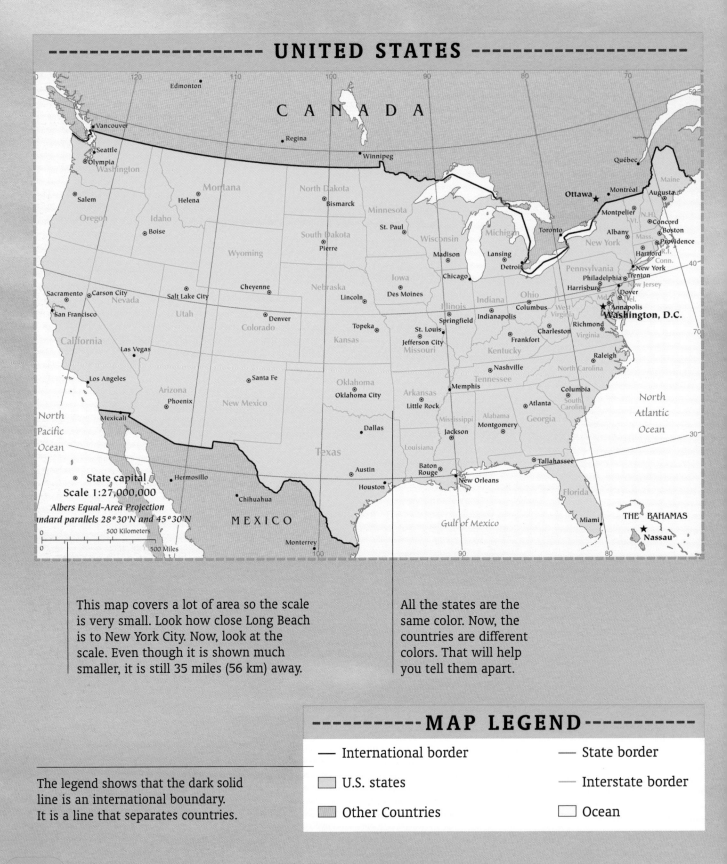

UNITED STATES

CANADA

Edmonton
Vancouver
Regina
Winnipeg
Seattle
Olympia
Washington
Salem
Montana
North Dakota
Minnesota
Québec
Helena
Bismarck
Ottawa
Montréal
Augusta
Maine
Oregon
Idaho
Boise
South Dakota
St. Paul
Wisconsin
Michigan
Toronto
Montpelier
N.H.
Concord
Boston
Vt.
Mass.
Sacramento
Carson City
Nevada
Salt Lake City
Wyoming
Pierre
Madison
Lansing
Detroit
New York
Albany
Providence
R.I.
Hartford
Conn.
Cheyenne
Nebraska
Iowa
Des Moines
Chicago
Illinois
Indiana
Ohio
Pennsylvania
Philadelphia
Harrisburg
New Jersey
Trenton
Dover
Del.
San Francisco
Utah
Colorado
Denver
Lincoln
Topeka
St. Louis
Springfield
Indianapolis
Columbus
West Virginia
Virginia
Richmond
Annapolis
Md.
Washington, D.C.
California
Las Vegas
Kansas
Jefferson City
Missouri
Frankfort
Charleston
Kentucky
Nashville
Raleigh
North Carolina
Los Angeles
Arizona
Santa Fe
Oklahoma
Oklahoma City
Arkansas
Little Rock
Memphis
Tennessee
Columbia
South Carolina
North Atlantic Ocean
Phoenix
New Mexico
Mississippi
Alabama
Georgia
Atlanta
North Pacific Ocean
Mexicali
Dallas
Texas
Jackson
Montgomery
Austin
Baton Rouge
Louisiana
Tallahassee
State capital
Scale 1:27,000,000
Albers Equal-Area Projection
Standard parallels 28°30'N and 45°30'N
Hermosillo
Houston
New Orleans
Florida
500 Kilometers
0
0
500 Miles
Chihuahua
MEXICO
Gulf of Mexico
Miami
THE BAHAMAS
Monterrey
Nassau

This map covers a lot of area so the scale is very small. Look how close Long Beach is to New York City. Now, look at the scale. Even though it is shown much smaller, it is still 35 miles (56 km) away.

All the states are the same color. Now, the countries are different colors. That will help you tell them apart.

The legend shows that the dark solid line is an international boundary. It is a line that separates countries.

MAP LEGEND

—— International border
☐ U.S. states
▨ Other Countries

— State border
— Interstate border
☐ Ocean

The map below shows more of Mexico and Canada. Read the map title. Now we know what the map is showing us: the continent of North America.

So, now you know where I am! I'm in my bedroom, in my house, in my neighborhood, in my city, in my state, in the United States, on the continent of North America! But where exactly is North America?

NORTH AMERICA

This map shows the cities of North America. The bigger the name of the city, the bigger the real city is.

Where in the World Am I?
Here on Earth!

North America is a continent on Earth. The world is not flat—you know that. But maps ARE flat. Maps are like opened **globes**. If you peeled the picture off a globe, and tried to lay it flat, you would have a map.

▼ A globe is a map, but it shows the whole world in its round form. Globes can be based on pictures of Earth, so they can be made exactly right. But you can't make a round ball on flat paper.

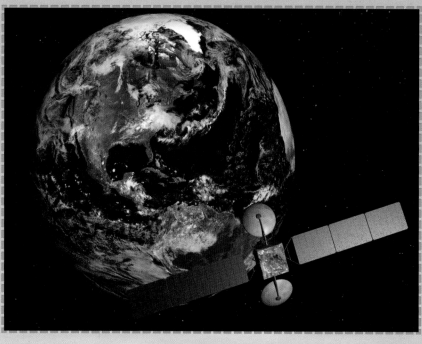

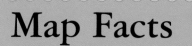 *Maps made this way are very popular. They are called **projection maps**.*

Projection maps are not always perfect. There are some mistakes in how big or where continents are. For example, this projection map cuts off part of Antarctica. It also makes Alaska and Russia look far apart. They are really close together!

Map Facts

No one knew that America existed when Columbus traveled here in 1492. He thought he had sailed to India.

▲ *Globes are shaped like a ball because Earth is shaped like a ball.*

The United States is a country in North America. You can see the continent below. Like small maps, this big map has a title: "Map of the World." That title tells you that this map will show you the location of the countries in the world.

World maps show lines that go all around Earth. Those are lines of **latitude**. The center line is the **equator**. The lines aren't really on Earth.

MAP OF THE WORLD

They just help people measure where places are. Each latitude line is a measure of how far north or south a place is from the equator.

World maps show lines going up and down Earth. Those are lines of **longitude**. Just like lines of latitude aren't really on Earth, neither are the lines of longitude. They tell how far east or west a place is.

Map Facts

Maps of the world change all the time. For example, when a country changes its name, maps need to change, too.

The closer to the equator you are, the warmer the weather usually is.

Africa is a continent. This map uses color to show the countries on the continent.

This is another world map, but its title is different: "Physical Map of the World." A **physical map** is a map that shows natural features, such as mountains, lakes, and rivers.

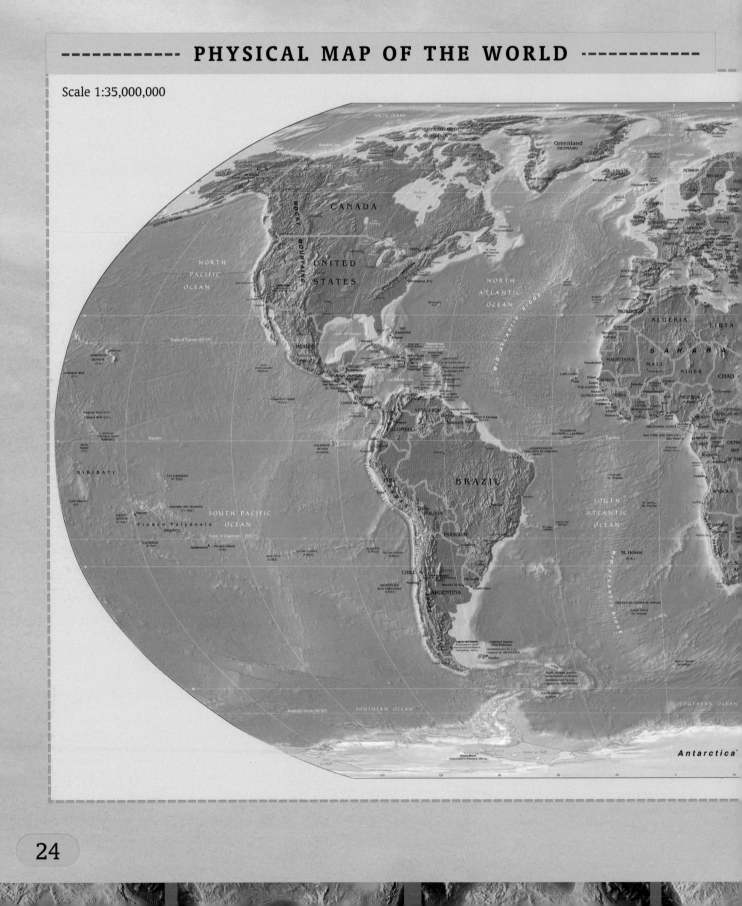

PHYSICAL MAP OF THE WORLD

Scale 1:35,000,000

Map Facts

There is land under the oceans, too. This is called the Mariana Trench. It is deeper than any other part of any ocean!

As the color on the land changes from green to tan, the land goes from flat to hilly. The colors on the land get lighter as the land turns into mountains.

Now, Africa's countries are not different colors. That's because this map doesn't show countries— it shows the shape of the land.

Even though this map uses color, the bodies of water are still blue. Water is blue on nearly all maps.

Finding Your Way in the World

No matter what a map tells you, all maps have some of the same map parts. They all have:
- a title to tell you what the map is about,
- a compass rose to tell you which way is north,
- a scale to show you how to read distance, and
- a legend to show you what each symbol means.

▼ *This is a picture of my classroom! But where is my desk?*

Well, let's look at these maps. Here is a map I made of my school campus. I think I will call it "West School Campus." Even though it is just a handmade map, it has all the parts that you need to read it.

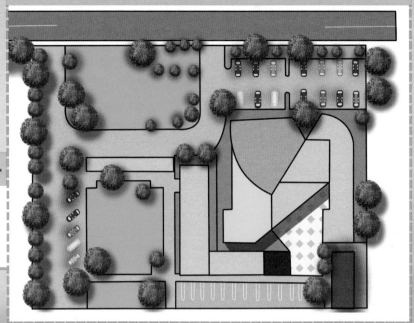

--- MAP LEGEND ---

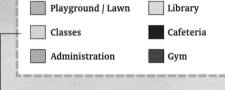

▨	Playground / Lawn	▢	Library
▢	Classes	■	Cafeteria
▨	Administration	▨	Gym

The legend shows where the playground, library, cafeteria, and gym are. Can you find each?

----------- MY DESK -----------

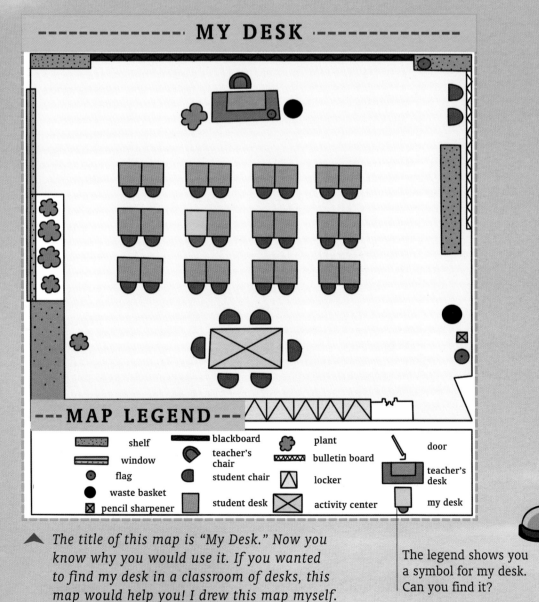

--- MAP LEGEND ---

▨ shelf	▬ blackboard	✿ plant		╱ door	
▭ window	◗ teacher's chair	▨ bulletin board		▭ teacher's desk	
◉ flag	◖ student chair	◻ locker		▯ my desk	
● waste basket	▨ student desk	⊠ activity center			
⊠ pencil sharpener					

▲ *The title of this map is "My Desk." Now you know why you would use it. If you wanted to find my desk in a classroom of desks, this map would help you! I drew this map myself.*

The legend shows you a symbol for my desk. Can you find it?

The two maps on this page are very different. But they both show Long Island!

Both maps have compass roses, titles, and symbols. Once you know your map parts, you will be able to read any map—no matter what it's trying to tell you.

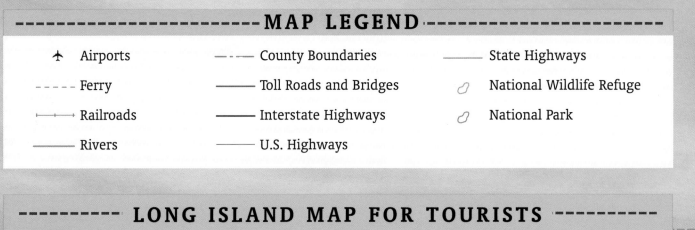

------------------------------ MAP LEGEND ------------------------------

✈ Airports	─ ∙ ─ County Boundaries	─── State Highways
- - - - - Ferry	─── Toll Roads and Bridges	⬭ National Wildlife Refuge
⊢─┼─⊣ Railroads	━━━ Interstate Highways	⬭ National Park
─── Rivers	─── U.S. Highways	

---------- LONG ISLAND MAP FOR TOURISTS ----------

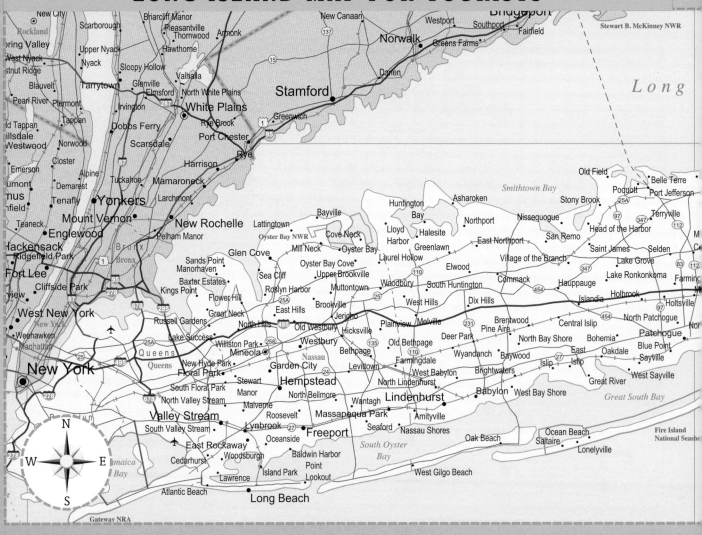

▲ *The title of this map is "Long Island Map for Tourists." Look at the legend. There are symbols for roads, ferries, and trains. This map must tell people how to get around Long Island.*

LIGHTHOUSES OF LONG ISLAND

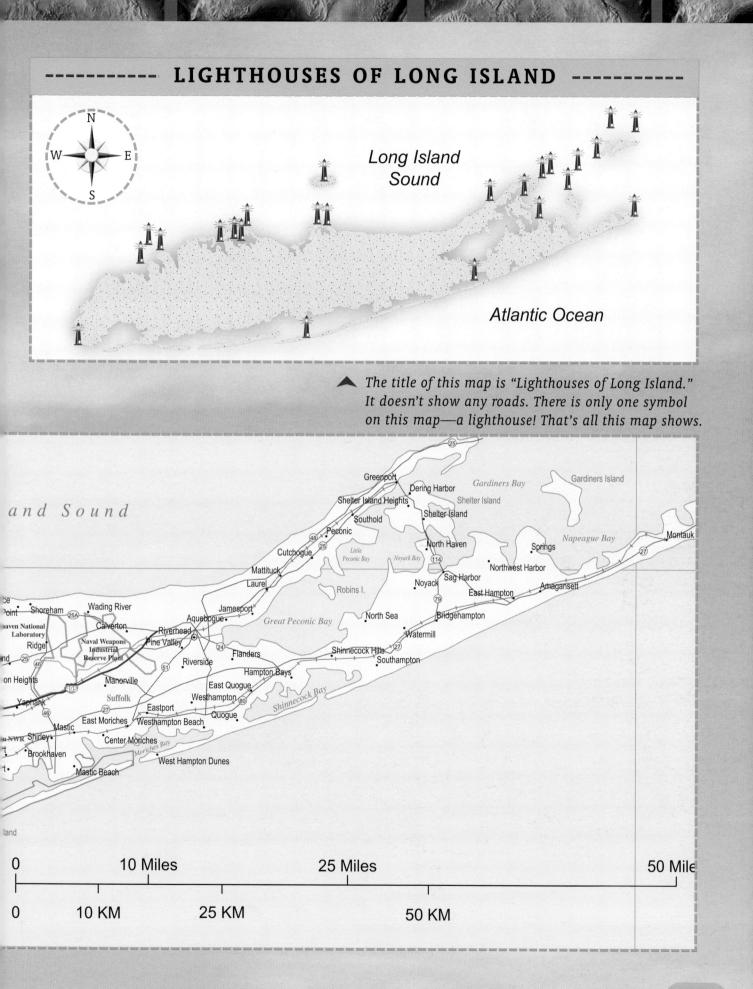

Long Island
Sound

Atlantic Ocean

▲ The title of this map is "Lighthouses of Long Island."
It doesn't show any roads. There is only one symbol
on this map—a lighthouse! That's all this map shows.

Greenport
Dering Harbor   Gardiners Bay   Gardiners Island
Shelter Island Heights
Southold   Shelter Island
and Sound   Peconic
Cutchogue   North Haven   Napeague Bay   Montauk
Mattituck   Little Peconic Bay   Noyack Bay   Springs
Laurel   Robins I.   Noyack   Northwest Harbor
Wading River   Jamesport   Sag Harbor   Amagansett
Point   Shoreham   Aquebogue   Great Peconic Bay   East Hampton
aaven National   Calverton   Riverhead   North Sea   Bridgehampton
Laboratory   Naval Weapons   Pine Valley
Ridge   Industrial   Flanders   Watermill
Reserve Plant   Riverside   Shinnecock Hills
on Heights   Manorville   Hampton Bays   Southampton
Yaphank   Suffolk   East Quogue
Mastic   Eastport   Westhampton   Quogue
East Moriches   Westhampton Beach
NWR Shirley   Center Moriches   Moriches Bay
Brookhaven   West Hampton Dunes
Mastic Beach

| 0 | 10 Miles | 25 Miles | 50 Mile |

| 0 | 10 KM | 25 KM | 50 KM |

So Here I Am!

Okay, so NOW do you know where I am?

▲ In my house...

▲ I am in my bedroom...

▲ In my neighborhood...

▲ In my city called Long Beach...

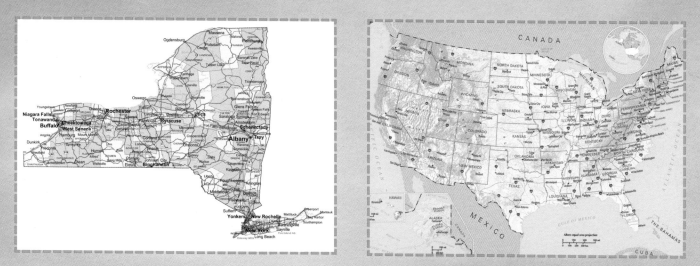

▲ In my state called New York...

▲ In the country called The United States...

▲ On the continent called North America and on the planet called EARTH!

Map Facts

Long ago, people sailed across oceans without maps. They watched the birds and stars to figure out where they were. When they came home, they made maps. Some are very exact.

Where in the world are YOU?

Glossary

Note: Some boldfaced words are defined where they appear in the book

boundaries Lines that show where one place ends and another begins

compass rose A map part that shows you which way on the map is north, south, east, and west

equator The line of latitude that circles the center of Earth from east to west

large scale map A map that shows a small area of land

latitude Lines on maps that are used to measure how far a place is from the equator

legend A key to decoding symbols on a map

longitude Lines on maps that are used to measure how far east or west a place is

scale A map part that shows you how to read distance on a map

small scale map A map that shows a large area of land

symbol A shape or color that represents a building, place, or other part on a map

title A map part that tells you what the map will show you

Index

Printed in the U.S.A. - CG